Beautiful Just Like Me

A Collaboration Led By

Regina Sunshine Robinson

Book 3 of the Awesome Girl Book Series

Published by the Regina Sunshine Global Network, LLC

Cover Design by Darshawne Wickerson
Character Design by Olivia Elizabeth Stanley
Editing by Pamelia Gore Stanley
Editing by Charlotte Ehney
Logo Design by Kristen Culbreath

For information:
Regina Sunshine Global Network, LLC
www.ReginaSunshine.com

ISBN: 978-1-7359384-5-5 Paperback
ISBN: 978-1-7359384-6-2 Ebook

AWESOME
GIRL

DEDICATION

She was one of the most beautiful people I have ever known. And I'm not just talking about the way she looked. She had a beautiful heart. I don't remember when we met. It's like I always knew her. I just remember she became one of the best friends I ever had. Most people who knew us in high school knew that but many don't know what she meant to me as an adult.

When Pam and I founded EWATE and decided to launch the Purpose Driven Women tour, she was the one who funded the start of the tour. I never asked for her help. She volunteered and planted a seed that led to the changed lives of thousands of women. She hosted events for us and was an active participant in many of our SASSY Women's Brunches. She was a true visionary.

Long before I was Regina Sunshine, she was my friend and one of the biggest supporters I ever had. The ripple effects of her words of encouragement, her love and her belief in me continue to fuel my work today. Without her, I wouldn't be where I am now.
So, I dedicate this book to Latonya Stephens Smith. The work you did on Earth continues to bring people to the Kingdom. Thank you for always setting the pace and being beautifully different. You are and will always be a big part of the mission of my life. Your presence is forever missed, but your legacy is strong. Until we meet again, I rejoice now in your "Well Done."

Regina Sunshine Robinson

TABLE OF CONTENTS

	ACKNOWLEDGEMENTS	
	INTRODUCTION	9
1	SOMMER DAINA BUTLER	12
2	KANURI ELISE FOWLER -YIKEALO	14
3	BAILEY DENISE BOYD	18
4	OLIVIA ELIZABETH STANLEY	20
5	DE'ZYRE WILLIAMS	24
6	SARAI LOKEY	28
7	ZAYDAH LOTALLAH	30
8	JOY MCKENZIE WRIGHT	34
9	JORDAN NEWKIRK	38
10	NESHIA MILTON	40
11	ZOE PATSY GORE	42
12	JAYDEN DION PUGH	44
	AWESOME GIRL POEM & AFFIRMATIONS	46
	LETTER TO AWESOME GIRL	49
	BOOK SPONSORS	52

"IT'S NOT OVER TIL YOU WIN!"

Regina Sunshine Robinson

INTRODUCTION

When we began planning the third book in our Awesome Girl Series, the title came to me immediately. I know it was sent to me for just this time. So much of what we believe about ourselves is related to our appearance. The world at large pays so much attention to our looks that many people, especially our girls, believe that's where their value lies. But how many of us know someone who is physically very attractive but whose heart is stone-cold? When we think of them or spend time with them, do we feel the beauty, or are we happy to get away from them? Maya Angelou once said, "People will forget what you said, but they will never forget how you made them feel."

Psalm 139:14 says we were "fearfully and wonderfully made." This speaks to our hearts not our faces or our bodies. When someone makes you feel good, that's beauty. When someone does good, that's beauty. When someone serves, gives, loves … that's beauty. And in a world that often teaches our girls that their outer appearance is the most important thing, we decided to give our Awesome Girls a chance to tell the world what they know beauty is. So, join us on this journey, this third adventure into the minds and hearts of some truly beautiful girls. I hope you are inspired and that you believe our girls when they say, "You Are Beautiful Just Like Me."

Remember this …

- God loves you just the way you are.
- You are beautiful because you were created in love.
- You are fearfully and wonderfully made.
- You have the seeds of greatness within you.
- You were born to live a victorious life.
- You are brilliant, gorgeous, talented, and fabulous.
- You are worthy of the best things in life.
- And one more thing … It's Not Over Til You Win!

AWESOME
GIRL

CHAPTER 1

SOMMER DAINA BUTLER

Age: 7

Beautiful Just Like Me

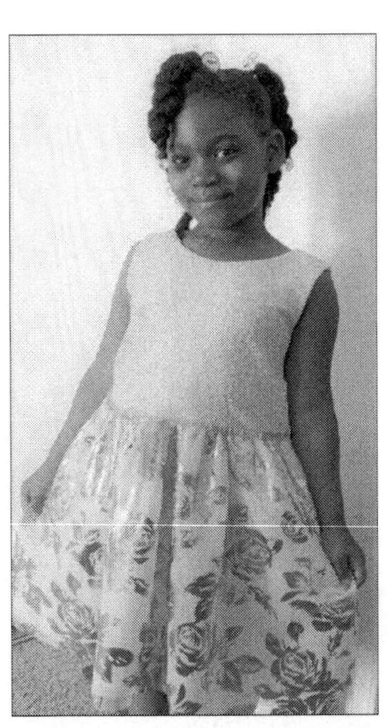

I believe beauty is from the inside and not the outside. Beauty comes from the inside of your heart and mind. I am beautiful, and this is why I love people and my dog Cesar. People are unique, smart, kind, and loving. People help other people by feeding them and giving them clothes. That's beauty from the inside. Helping people is beautiful. Making people happy feels good. Everyone should be good and feeling good is beautiful. You have to be nice to be beautiful. To truly be beautiful you should stay positive and always believe in yourself.

"Be strong, be fearless, be beautiful."
-Misty Copeland

Affirmations

1. I am beautiful inside and out.
2. When I look in the mirror, I see beauty.
3. My hair is beautiful just like me.
4. The more positive I am the more beautiful I become.
5. I am an awesome swimmer.

Bio

Sommer Butler, daughter of Crystal Brown and Dainhen Butler, is 7 years old and attends CJ Hicks Elementary. In her spare time, she enjoys sewing, swimming, painting, skating, gardening, and cooking what she grows. Sommer aspires to be a dentist and an Olympic swimmer.

CHAPTER 2

KANURI ELISE FOWLER-YIKEALO

Age: 9

Beautiful Just Like Me

I have learned in life that beauty and what is beautiful is different to each of us. Looking around, you will see nature as beautiful in its art form. An example of beauty in my eyes is my little cousin, Liv. Liv is 6 years old and is beautiful inside and out. She can dance, sing, and do gymnastics. Her smile is a ray of sunlight. She is what is beautiful to me, as well as having many great qualities still growing inside her.

Before I begin to speak of my beauty, there is another person dear to me who is an example of beauty. Each day from the time I can remember, my mom has been my definition of beauty. Daily, I am reminded of how she nurtures and cares for me with endless love. Her beauty can also be seen in how I care for others. Also, she makes sure that my mind is enriched by giving me experiences to help me grow even when I resist sometimes. I can count on her to remind me of the importance of rest, so I will have the strength to endure the challenges of the day. She encourages me to take care of my body by putting me in activities such as dance, art, Girl Scouts, and singing. Mom makes sure I am around people who can bring the best out in me or challenge me. She reminds me to ask myself, "What is your why?"

Socially, my family, friends, and others help me to develop and grow. I see myself as one of God's creations. God allows me each day to experience Him in nature. I can listen to the wind blow, birds sing, and water running over the rocks. This is God's gift of beauty in the world that I can see.

I can see myself in the life and actions of my mom and cousin-sister, Liv. Looking deeply into myself, I can see my beauty because of beautiful people who have made and are making a way for me. This community of beauty is different to all who experience it. Through my eyes, this is beautiful. I feel the most beautiful when I am laughing and having fun with my mom, family and friends. My mom has taught me not to be all about things and stuff, but to learn how to turn lemon into lemonade for myself and others. When I look outward at others, my beauty can be seen as how I treat people and make them feel. When I look at my beauty, I can see all of those examples of beauty mentioned in the words above. Yes, my beauty begins within me and how others experience me in my family, in friends, and in community.

As you can see, I can find beauty in the very small of God's creations with my beloved mom and others, but most of all I find beauty in me!

Affirmations

1. I love myself.
2. I'm glad God made me.

3. I am so good.
4. I am beautiful.
5. I love Mommy and Mommy loves me.

Bio

Kanuri Elise Fowler-Yikealo is nine years old and attends Providence Christian School. She is the daughter of Dr. Jillian Whatley and Oluyemi Fowler-Yikealo. Kanuri is a member of Girl Scouts, Diamond In the Rough Youth Development Program, Dance Phusion (ballet and tap), and she takes voice lessons. Her future dreams include developing a YouTube Channel focusing on animations and games, becoming a famous singer, and feeding the homeless. Kanuri has a passion for helping homeless people and providing them with food, so they won't be hungry.

"You don't have to stay in the dark and hide in the shadows of life. Get out there and be free, girl, to do what you want and be what you want to be."- Kanuri Elise Fowler-Yikealo.

CHAPTER 3

BAILEY DENISE BOYD

Age: 10

Beautiful Just Like Me

I am beautiful because God made only one Bailey Denise Boyd, just like He created one version of you. Celebrate the idea that you are uniquely created, and there is no other copy of you in the whole world. Think about just how special that really is.

Everyone in the world is beautiful in God's eyes simply because He made everyone. If you do not feel beautiful, this is what you need to know … God and your family love you more than you can ever imagine. Like God's angels, we have to love each other and God's beautiful works. So, no matter how small or big, we are all important and have a specific purpose. We are like flowers in a garden all waiting to blossom and bloom when the time is right … and that is BEAUTIFUL!

Affirmations

1. The most beautiful person in the world is my mom, and it is because she has the perfect personality.
2. Beauty is in the way we treat other people with respect.
3. If you don't feel beautiful, you need to know that your family and God love you.
4. You are beautiful because you are your own person, in your own way, and that is special.
5. God made us different and unique.

Bio

Bailey Denise Boyd is the daughter of Billy and Diana Boyd. Her dad is a police officer and her mom is a nurse. She has a twin brother named Ethan and they are both ten old years old. She has an older brother named Caden, and he is really good in basketball. Bailey likes to play on the iPad and watch dance videos on YouTube. She loves playing the game Roblox, as well as reading books by Judy Moody and the Diary of a Wimpy Kid series. Bailey likes to play outside with her friends. When she gets older, she wants to be a dance teacher.

CHAPTER 4

OLIVIA ELIZABETH STANLEY

Age: 10

Different Shades of Beauty

I am beautiful! My brown skin, big brown eyes, and big hair are just some things that make me beautiful. Beauty is not just what you can see with your eyes. Being kind, loving, smart, giving, and having a joyful heart are also things that make me beautiful. What you do and who you are both are equally important.

I believe butterflies are beautiful. Each one has a unique design. Sunsets, waterfalls, and flowers are things I believe are beautiful in the world. Some people are like flowers. They have different personalities and different talents. People, like flowers, are unique in their own way. Like flowers, some people are known for their beauty while others are known for what they offer to the world.

Some things I see beauty in that others may not are cloudy days. Some people feel sad or in a certain mood when it is cloudy outside. Cloudy days are relaxing to me. I also find beauty in simple things like watching rain fall.

Beautiful people change the world. The most beautiful person in the world was my great grandmother, Elizabeth Alford. She taught my mom how to sew and Mom taught me. Great Grandmother Elizabeth was kind and caring. She was gentle. She always made sure that everyone was taken care of and happy. The things that I have learned from her I will continue to use throughout my life.

I believe everyone has something beautiful about them. God put all of us on earth with a purpose. I believe I can make the world more beautiful by using my gifts and talents to help others. I can sew coats and give them to homeless people during the winter. I can plant a garden and feed people who need food to eat. Most importantly, I can spend time with people so they do not feel alone, and they know someone cares about them.

It is important for me to dream and be beautiful. The world needs me along with other beautiful people to become a better place. So, in the words of Coco Chanel, "Keep your heels, head, and standards high." Olivia Stanley is going to be Legendary!

Affirmations

1. I trust in God, I have faith in God, and I expect God!
2. I am an Awesome Girl!
3. Never be afraid because God is with you!
4. I am beautiful, bold, and brave!
5. I am going to be Legendary!

Bio

Olivia Elizabeth Stanley was born in Cary, NC on March 25, 2011. She is the daughter of Oliver and Pamelia Stanley. She is a published author and illustrator. She is also an owner and designer at OES Designs where she makes doll clothing and accessories. Her goal when she grows up is to be Legendary!

CHAPTER 5

DE'ZYRE WILLIAMS

Age: 10

Beautiful Just Like Me

My name is De'Zyre (pronounced desire). The word "desire" is synonymous to being of greatness, worthiness, magnificence, and uniqueness. I am beautiful because God made me beautiful. My beauty was instilled in me by God in order to inspire myself and other girls to strive for what they dream to do in life and to be themselves. You are beautiful because you are unique and full of dreams just like me. It does not matter if you want to be a doctor, singer, hairdresser, or even an author. Whatever you want to do in life, you can achieve it by working hard and believing just how beautiful you are.

To begin with, you are beautiful just like me because everyone is beautiful in their own way. Never listen to those who have negative energy because God made everyone uniquely and individually beautiful. I believe that beauty is from within, meaning that it is what is on the inside of a person's heart that matters most. To illustrate this, the most beautiful person in the world to me is my mother because she means the world to me. She is a single mother, college professor, and mental health worker. My mother is such a magnificent and beautiful person because she is always willing to help others who may need assistance with anything, such as navigating through resources or giving them her last to see them fulfill their aspirations.

Moreover, if you do not feel beautiful, you need to know that there is a community of people around you who can help you see that you are gorgeous just the way you are. You do not have to change yourself for anyone else. Beauty is the way that we treat others and the way that people treat you. God sees us as beautiful and beloved. If anyone tells you anything negative or that you are not beautiful, it is because you are excelling and living in your purpose that God has designed just for you. God has made all of us equally with the intention for us to love one another and to continue to make this world beautiful.

In closing, I want to leave you with this nugget of beauty. Always remember that beauty can be found anywhere in the world. Never think that your appearance, the negative energy from people, or the mistakes that you have made cause you not to be beautiful. I like to think that false appearance, negative energy, and mistakes are beauty marks. Beauty marks are the dark spots in your life that taught you to become a greater you … a BEAUTIFUL you! Never look down upon yourself! Always stand up straight, tall, chin up, and say "I am a beautiful girl!"

Affirmation

1. You are beautiful.
2. Never give up.
3. Always be yourself.
4. Don't listen to haters.
5. Dream big.

Bio

De'Zyre Williams is a 10 year old from Northeastern North Carolina. She has been a published author and entrepreneur since she was 6 years old. Learn more about De'Zyre, purchase any of her books, or book her for speaking engagements/book signings on her website at www.dezyrewilliams.com, by email at dezyrewilliamsenterprises@gmail.com or by phone at 757.354.1177.

CHAPTER 6

SARAI LOKEY

Age: 11

What Makes You Beautiful

Your beauty doesn't come from the outside, it comes from the inside. What makes you beautiful? I believe my willingness to help those in need, my thoughtfulness towards others, and my love for others make me beautiful. You may not have the same reasons I do that make you beautiful and that's ok! God made us each in our own way. We're all different but we're all God's children. God loves us and knew what He was doing when He made us. A lot of things can make you beautiful whether it's your caring heart, kindness, thoughtfulness, patience, and more! Don't sell yourself short! You are wonderfully and creatively made by God! Do you sometimes feel like you are not beautiful? The Bible in the chapter of Ephesians 1 says what God says YOU ARE! You are CHOSEN, you are REDEEMED, you are FORGIVEN, you are LOVED, and so much more. God loves and cares for us and doesn't want us to think for a second we are not beautiful! God is an intelligent God that made us differently but loves us all the same! God loves us just the way we are and doesn't want us to change who he created us to be. Have you ever felt that you had to change the way you are just to fit in? I know that feeling. Every once in a while, you can get caught up in the world and want to change who you are just to fit in! You may think that everyone would love your new change, right? NO, that's not true! God wouldn't like your new change and neither would you!! We were created to be a Godly human example of Him in every step we take! Also, you wouldn't enjoy your made-up self either because for so long you were this person you loved being and then suddenly you changed to fit in. It's hard to change from somebody you were into something you suddenly became. I advise you to not get so caught up in the world that you lose who you are. Who you are is special! Why? Well, because there is ONLY ONE YOU! Stay true to yourself and don't change for other people's approval. If you have to transform and grow, make sure it's only for the glory of God's kingdom!

Affirmations

1. I'm beautiful just the way I am.
2. I'm capable of anything if I work hard.
3. I'm smart.
4. I'm unique.
5. I'm intelligent.

Bio

Sarai Lokey is eleven years old. She lives with her sister, mom, dad, and dog named "Sugar". Sarai loves hanging out with friends, reading books, and being with her family.

CHAPTER 7

ZAYDAH LOTALLAH

Age: 12

What Makes Beauty

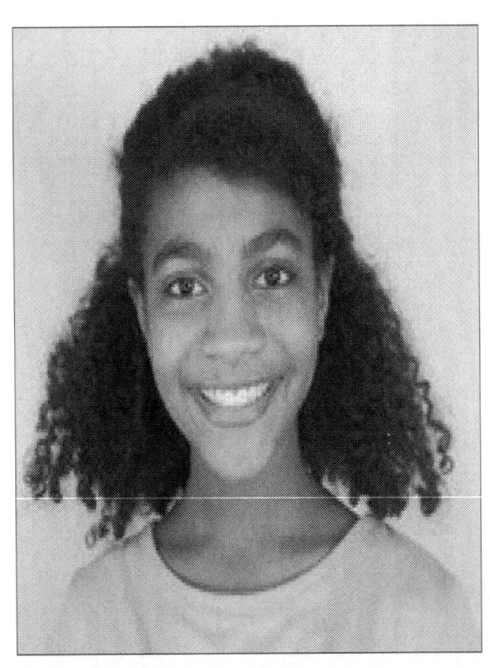

What makes beauty? Who decides what beauty is or when you feel beautiful? Beauty often seems hard to achieve, and it has so many very different definitions! You may feel lost in the search for beauty. As humans, we might look in the wrong places. Well, I am here to tell you that the search is over. All the beauty in the world is inside of you! Yes YOU, the gorgeous person reading these words. You see, beauty isn't how you look or how other people look at you. Beauty is the way you look at yourself; you're a person with talents beyond the world's knowledge. When I think of you, I know you are beautiful, from the way you walk to the way you conduct yourself with others. Other people have standards for their form of beauty, but you don't have to worry about theirs. You only need to worry about the standards you set for yourself. Be true to you!

A lot of times when people create standards for others, it's because they are lost. But once you start to see your love for yourself, you begin to be found! When you find yourself, you become comfortable in your own skin, and that sparks an undeniable confidence.

Yeah, confidence. It starts on the inside and begins to shine throughout everything you do. There is nothing more beautiful than being your own unique self. Never second-guess your beauty. If it feels right, it's you. You have to know that you already are everything you want to be! Everyone has something that makes them special and different. If you are struggling to feel the beauty that is inside of you, then you use what makes you special to inspire self-love and confidence. People who you look up to can also help you feel your beauty! Think about what you have in common with them and how that makes you beautiful as well.

So back to the original question: What makes beauty?

You make beauty. Everything you do is beautiful. You are a gorgeous person on the inside, and it makes you shine in an undeniable way! You create beauty's definition when you decide when and why you feel beautiful. You have a gorgeous soul. So, love it, as it will teach you how to soar.

Affirmations

1. I am everything I want to be.
2. I am happy.
3. I am beauty.
4. I love myself.
5. I fulfill my dreams.

Bio

Zaydah Lotallah is a speaker, actress, singer, and author all while independently homeschooling. Zaydah hopes to use these public skills and platforms to make the world a better place, especially in the areas of social justice and civil rights. Her greatest dream is to be a lawyer who finds new ways to create positive change. While not in law school yet, she lives just outside of Atlanta, GA with her parents and two younger brothers.

Connect with Zaydah via her email at zlotallah@gmail.com, see what she's up to on YouTube @Zaydah Love, or check out her slime shop on Instagram @diaphanousslimes.

CHAPTER 8

JOY MCKENZIE WRIGHT

Age: 13

Beauty Always Finds A Way To Break Through The Ugly

I believe beauty is from the inside because ... beauty is not about your clothes, shoes or how popular you are to other people. Beauty is not about how you look, smell or how much you weigh. Beauty is not your sex, gender, religious beliefs or even the color of your skin. Beauty to me is and will always be how we treat one another. My mother often says, "Beauty is an inward design that manifests itself in our outward service to humanity." That is what I believe the true description of beauty is. It is what you are truly made of and how we show up in the world.

You can find beauty in so many things like nature, flowers, animals, people, pictures and the wonderful breeze in the spring. But none of these natural wonders mean anything if they are not properly treated to become the most beautiful things on our planet. This is the same in humanity. People come in all forms. When we don't show people love and care then their beauty is neglected, and we as a people miss the wonderful opportunity to see the beauty in each one of us.

There are so many girls in the world who think that they are ugly because of their skin, race, gender, sex, hair, weight and body features. What they don't realize is that none of these things matter at all. The truth is that the only thing that matters is that we treat people with love, dignity and respect; that is true beauty. It is just like the big tree in my back yard. It's not the prettiest tree in the yard but it is the home of beautiful birds, squirrels, insects, and so much more. The beauty is not the tree itself; the beauty is what the tree offers the animal kingdom.

Beauty is from the inside because service and having the heart to stand up for all that is right make the world a beautiful place. Activists who protest for Black Lives Matter, the LGBTQ community, the environment and the many other people who fight for the voiceless and poor people in our world are beautiful. Beauty to me is the fight for equality and the rise of a whole new generation that is going to change the world.

And although the world has taken so many dark turns with slavery, segregation, women's rights, war, politics and police brutality, beauty still lives on. Beauty always finds a way to break through the ugly. Beauty still lives on in the history of black women like Oprah Winfrey; Simone Biles; Serena and Venus Williams; Dorothy Height; civil rights activist Daisy Bates; and Ethel Hedgeman Lyle, one of the founders of Alpha Kappa Alpha Sorority Inc., the first African American Sorority. This kind of beauty is true today. It can be seen in the hard work and dedication from mentors like Ms. Regina "Sunshine" Robinson who has inspired me to reach beyond the stars and my mother who teaches me to use my power to build up other girls in my world and not tear them down.

There is one thing I truly know; although I am only thirteen years old, I know beauty when I see it. I know that anyone can put on a pair of lashes or wear an expensive pair of shoes. But it takes courage and true beauty to serve someone other than yourself. Beauty is in the inside because it is a living part of everything. God created beauty for all of us. We just have to open our eyes to see it.

Affirmations

No One will ever …

1. TAKE away my Joy.
2. LOVE me like I love myself.
3. MAKE me feel less than I deserve.
4. KEEP me from making my dreams come true.
5. SEE my beauty with closed eyes.

Bio

Joy Wright is an advocate for change, empowering young girls in the foster care system and promoting young entrepreneurship through civil activism, literacy awareness, and story sharing. She is also the founder of Share Joy Give Hugs and co-author in the Awesome Girls Book Series. To find out more about Joy, go to ww.sharejoygivehugs.com.

CHAPTER 9

JORDAN NEWKIRK

Age: 14

Beautiful Just Like Me

I am beautiful, and this is why. I am beautiful because I care for other people in many different ways. I bring light to dark situations, and I always find a way to make people smile. I am beautiful because of my heart. I am always willing to do things in any situation. I also believe you can find beauty in many different places. I find beauty in dark places. For example, I found beauty during quarantine. I started a tie-dye business during quarantine, Jordesigns, and I have found so much beauty in it. I also started another business after my tie-dye business, Smoothies and a Story a day with Jay, where I would make a smoothie and read a story on the internet every day. It brought so much joy and beauty to not only me but many other people. I got sponsored by other small businesses around my area, and I got so much support for both of my businesses. I believe that beauty is everywhere, you just have to find it. I believe I can make the world more beautiful by radiating my positivity and light into the world. I can also use my business to help radiate positivity into the world. I can make people happy by reading uplifting books with encouraging affirmations. I can use my tie-dye to put happy colors and pretty designs into the world. You can be "Beautiful Just Like Me" if you use your light to bring joy to people. You could use your positivity to make people happy because I believe that everyone finds beauty in something. Beauty is endless so whenever you feel like there is no more beauty or joy in something, just remember there always is. You are beautiful, I am beautiful, and everything around us is beautiful!

Affirmation

1. I am a soldier.
2. I am beautiful and brilliant.
3. I have so much potential.
4. I surround myself with positivity.
5. I am enough.

Bio

Jordan Newkirk is a 14 year old rising sophomore! She is a varsity cheerleader and a member of her school's dance team! Jordan is the owner of Jordesigns, a tie-dye business she started during the quarantine. You can find her on Instagram @shopjordesigns!

CHAPTER 10

NESHIA MILTON

Age: 16

Beautiful Just Like Me

Being beautiful can mean a lot of things. There are many forms of beauty. But when it comes down to it the essence of beauty is all the same, whether a rose glistening from morning dew or a beautiful black girl getting her hair done. Beauty can be found anywhere, in animals and humans doing the simplest of things. Personally, I believe one of the most important forms of beauty is inner beauty. It's so important because it's the beauty that you can't exactly see. People tend to only really worry about what they can see, and disregard what they can't; but focusing on what you can't see is just as, if not more, important than focusing on what you can see. The trail to finding your inner beauty is one of self-love and confidence. It is knowing your worth and knowing where you stand even in the face of other people who seek to tear you down. You must know that no one can determine or take your beauty away. It's an uphill battle, but definitely one that must be fought. Do not forget to trust yourself. Know that you are worthy of love and affection, and that you are beauty personified.

Affirmations

1. I am incredibly beautiful; makeup is just my power up.
2. Today will be an amazing day, I will smile brightly, and I will do my best to make others smile.
3. I love everything about myself: my body, my intellect, my courage and my shine.
4. I cannot control the people around me, but I can control myself, and that is enough for me.
5. I am more than enough, for myself and for others; I will not change for other people, only for myself and for good.

Bio

Neshia Milton is an aspiring actress/singer with a passion to entertain. She wants to leave behind something that's going to help people smile with the time God's gifted her on earth. Currently she is performing in musicals and plays but would love to branch out. Her main social is Instagram, and her handle is Marshy_Del_Taco. Be on the lookout for her on the big screen!

CHAPTER 11

ZOE PATSY GORE

Age: 17

Beautiful Just Like Me

There are girls who are beautiful just like me. I know many girls want to find their beauty. To find your beauty, you first have to accept yourself and love yourself. Girls and women as well, look at yourself and accept who you are and the beauty that's within you. A lot of girls don't accept their beauty because they are different. Listen here, your differences also make your beauty. Do not be ashamed to be different because the things you might not see as beauty other people see as unique and real, true beauty. God made us all. In his word in Psalm 139:14 it says, "I will praise thee; for I am fearfully and wonderfully made: Marvelous are thy works; And that my soul knoweth right well." So, with that being said, God made you just the way you are. Appreciate the works God did with you. To the girls who think because you don't fit in you are not beautiful, please stop thinking that because you are not made to fit into some things. The things you don't fit into are the things that make you stand out and shine. Beauty doesn't always come from what's on the outside. Beauty comes from within yourself. And wherever you go, smile. Keep your head up. Walk like you are proud to be who you are. Girls, women, and young women who you may never know are watching you. You never know the change that you are making in other people's lives by smiling and being proud of who you are. The affirmations below are some tips on how to love and accept your beauty.

Affirmations

1. When you wake up, say a positive thing to yourself.
2. Love yourself.
3. Accept who you are as a person.
4. Have a positive mindset and be happy.
5. Set a goal that you want to accomplish each day.

Bio

Zoe Patsy Gore is the daughter of Thomas Earl and Geraldine Gore and is the youngest of five girls. She is an eleventh grader at South Columbus High School in Tabor City, NC and attends Mitchell Sea Missionary Baptist Church in Green Sea, SC. Zoe enjoys singing in the church choir, being a part of the praise and worship team and dancing on the church praise team. Zoe also enjoys working with the youth at Finklea Community Center. She plans to attend North Carolina A&T State University to pursue a career as a psychologist.

CHAPTER 12

JAYDEN DION PUGH

Age: 17

Beautiful Just Like Me

I am beautiful because I have a kind heart, and I'm resilient. Beauty is about what's on the inside and how you treat others, not the outside or how you look. It is important to understand that concept. I believe that your imperfections make you beautiful. They make you unique and different. This helps you stand out in the world and makes you beautiful in your own way. My dreams are beautiful because doing what you love and what makes you happy is a beautiful thing. I feel beautiful when I embrace my insecurities and differences in the world instead of trying to hide them. I believe that it's okay to be yourself and be comfortable in your own skin. It's important to be confident in who you are and not worry about what others think because you are perfect just the way you are. Beauty comes from within, not your appearance or the way you look.

Affirmations

1. I am a beautiful woman.
2. My beauty is the greatest gift.
3. The more I love myself, the more beautiful I become.
4. I have a great sense of style, and it shows in what I wear and how I represent myself.
5. I am worthy.

Bio

Jayden Dion Pugh is 17 years old and lives in Los Angeles, California. She is an artist and enjoys making music (singing, songwriting, and producing) and making visual art. Her email is jaydendpugh@gmail.com. Contact her on Instagram, Facebook, TikTok, and Twitter @jaydenpughmusic.

Official Awesome Girl Poem

When you see her know that she is Awesome.
So Awesome she blossoms like a flower.
She has power and stands tall like a tower.
She was built to empower.
When you see her know that she is Awesome.

Her beauty comes from within,
Just where it's always been.
She's motivated to reach new heights,
Removing all obstacles with love, power and might.
When you see her know that she is Awesome.

The girl with the big dreams,
Who chases after them by all means,
Determined, motivated, elevated all in one,
Everything she does will pay off in the long run.
When you see her know that she is Awesome.

A girl who knows her worth,
Chosen for this journey from birth,
She lets her inner light shine,
And gets better each mountain she climbs.
When you see her know that she is Awesome.

She's your next doctor, lawyer, author, scholar.
She's the next Maya Angelou or Madame CJ Walker.
She's full of fire,
Someone you can admire.
She'll inspire the world.
She's one phenomenal girl.
When you see her know that she is Awesome.

Written by: AnTonia Williams
www.AnToniaMFWilliams.com

Regina Sunshine's Awesome Girl Affirmations

I was born to win.

I am more than a conqueror.

I was created for greatness.

I was born to be victorious.

I will achieve my dreams.

I can be anything I choose.

I can do anything I set my mind to.

I am a champion.

I am worthy of the best things in life.

I am worthy of the dreams in my heart.

I am worthy of living a great life.

I AM AN AWESOME GIRL.

A Letter from Regina to You, Awesome Girl!

From My Heart to Yours,

When I think of all the beauty in the world, my first thoughts are of you. What a beautiful time it is to be a girl. Your creativity, your heart and your uniqueness are the things that set you apart and not only make you an Awesome Girl but also simply beautiful. Continue to be you. Let all that you are shine bright and make the world an even more beautiful place. Use your gifts, talents, abilities and dreams to create an even more wonderful world for yourself and so many others. I hope you know that I'm proud to have you in our Awesome Girl family. Let's join forces to be the love, life and light to inspire all the girls we know to believe they are Beautiful Just Like You!

Be Blessed. Keep Winning!

Regina Sunshine

Author: ______________________________

Age: ______________________________

Beautiful Just Like Me:

Affirmations

1. ____

____

2. ____

____

3. ____

____

4. ____

____

5. ____

____

6. ____

____

7. ____

____

8. ____

____

9. ____

____

10. ____

____

BOOK SPONSOR

SHOE FETISH MOVEMENT

The Shoe Fetish Movement encourages and supports girls and women to know their self-worth, increase self-esteem through self-awareness, and gain confidence . . . an empowerment meeting/seminar with a flair. These qualities enable people to make better life choices, and stronger women mean stronger communities. Contact us for your next speaking event/meeting, 888-321-9604.

BOOK SPONSOR

FLO ENTERTAINMENT LLC

FLO Entertainment LLC understands the importance of creating a strong brand for its clients. FLO's mission is to develop and support clients so that their true potential is achieved. Our management company focuses on the management and support needs of our clients. We work hand in hand with clients to help guide and push them to greater heights.

Visit:

https://floentertainmentgroup.com for more details.

BOOK SPONSOR

DIAPHANOUS SLIMES

What makes us special? We are a small handmade business that provides a special selection of slimes with many different textures. We provide our products at an affordable price for a great product. Our business is about supporting dreams like being able to afford college.

What these slimes will do for you: they will help you to relax and remain calm. This is an awesome sensory toy and we provide a variety of different textures. This also helps if you are working on improving fine motor skills after an accident.

BOOK SPONSOR

POSITIVELY YOURS

Feel positively YOUR BEST!
sherrythompson.le-vel.com/thrivesamples/

Sherry Cockerham Thompson, Ed.S., is a former community college counselor/administrator with over 20 years of experience helping students achieve their dreams. She herself was once a non-traditional college student, having returned to college at the age of 30 when she was a single mom with three small boys under the age of five. As she helped students work towards achieving their dreams, she always remembered what it was like to be a scared college freshman living well below the poverty line. The road to that first, two-year degree was hard, but she believed her education was a way out of poverty for her and her children. She struggled, working part-time and going to school full-time, but she knew that someday she could help other women and make a difference in her community. Thompson now is an entrepreneur and enjoys helping others pursue their dreams through her writing and entrepreneurship. Her message now: DREAM BIG AND NEVER GIVE UP!!

BOOK SPONSOR

CREATE YOUR LEGACY LLC

Create Your Legacy LLC is a company founded by Gabriel Robinson in 2021. The purpose behind this company is within the name. We desire to maximize the potential of customers, business partners, and people we come in contact with through various business ventures. From Inspirational Apparel to Youth Empowerment, Martial Arts to Economic Development, we are striving to leave a positive legacy and assist others in doing the same. For more information or to partner with us, contact us at createyourlegacy2021@gmail.com.

AWESOME GIRL ACADEMY
AWESOME GIRL
REGINA SUNSHINE GLOBAL NETWORK

RSGN
REGINA SUNSHINE GLOBAL NETWORK

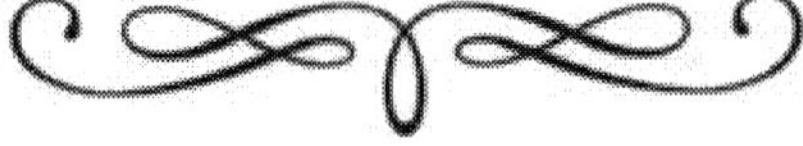

ABOUT THE CURATOR

Regina Sunshine Robinson is an author, motivational speaker, talk show host, empowerment coach, corporate trainer, and teacher. She is the CEO of the Regina Sunshine Global Network, parent company to everything Regina Sunshine including EWATE, a Women's Empowerment Organization whose main purpose is to empower and encourage women to be all they were created to be in order to fulfill God's perfect plan for their lives. She is also the founder of the Awesome Girl Academy. Regina's personal motto is "It's Not Over Til I Win" and she wins when she sees others "WINNING." For more information, go to ReginaSunshine.com.

Made in the USA
Middletown, DE
23 September 2021